Take-Home Leveled Readers

Below-level

Science

Editorial Offices: Glenview, Illinois • Parsippany, New Jersey • New York, New York
Sales Ofices: Needham, Massachusetts • Duluth, Georgia • Glenview, Illinois
Coppell, Texas • Sacramento, California • Mesa, Arizona

PEARSON

Scott
Foresman

sfsuccessnet.com

ISBN: 0-328-19718-1

Table of Contents

To the Teacher

Scott Foresman provides three Leveled Readers for every chapter of *Scott Foresman Science*, Grades 1–6: a *Below-Level Leveled Reader*, an *On-Level Leveled Reader*, and an *Advanced Leveled Reader*.

All three readers teach the same science concepts, same vocabulary, address the same target reading skill and contain the same graphic organizer as the corresponding student edition chapter, just at three different reading levels—providing access to important science content for all students. The On-level and Advanced readers also use additional examples to enrich the chapter and extend ideas

This book contains reproducible copies of the Below-Level Leveled Readers for Grade 1. These are designed for you to reproduce and send home with your students as appropriate. Encourage students to share these books with parents or family members in order to practice reading skills and reinforce science content.

Online versions of these and other readers are also available through the Scott Foresman Leveled Reader Database.

Living and Nonliving

by Zachary Cohn

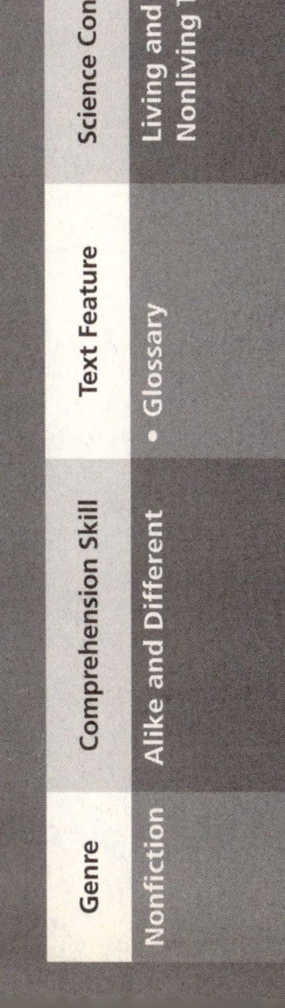

Genre	Comprehension Skill	Text Feature	Science Content
Nonfiction	Alike and Different	• Glossary	Living and Nonliving Things

Scott Foresman Science 1.1

PEARSON
Scott Foresman

scottforesman.com

ISBN 0-328-13733-2

9 780328 137336

What did you learn?

1. What do living things do?

2. What is a nonliving thing from nature?

3. **Writing** in Science Toys are nonliving things. Write to explain why they are nonliving. Use words from the book as you write.

4. **Alike and Different** How are plants and animals alike? How are plants and animals different?

Photographs: Every effort has been made to secure permission and provide appropriate credit for photographic material. The publisher deeply regrets any omission and pledges to correct errors called to its attention in subsequent editions. Unless otherwise acknowledged, all photographs are the property of Scott Foresman, a division of Pearson Education. Photo locators denoted as follows: Top (T), Center (C), Bottom (B), Left (L), Right (R) Background (Bkgd)
Title Page: Corbis 2 ©Darrell Gulin/Corbis 3 ©Pat O'Hara/Corbis 4 ©Photowood Inc./Corbis 5 ©J. & B. Photographers/Animals Animals/Earth Scenes 6 ©Roy Morsch/Corbis 7 ©Guy Edwardes/Getty Images 8 ©Darrell Gulin/Corbis 9 ©Dan Guravich/Corbis 10 ©Mary Kate Denny/PhotoEdit 12 ©DK Images 13 ©DK Images 14 (CC) Brand X Pictures, (CR) ©Guy Edwardes/Getty Images 15 (B) Corbis

ISBN: 0-328-13733-2

Copyright © Pearson Education, Inc.

Glossary

living   alive and can grow and change

nonliving   never alive

shelter   a safe place

Living and Nonliving

by Zachary Cohn

What are living things?

Plants are **living** things.

Animals are living things.

People are living things too.

What are some living things?

What are some nonliving things?

Water is a nonliving thing.

It does not grow.

It does not need food.

Nonliving things are in nature.

The butterfly is a living thing.

Plants and Animals

Plants grow.

Plants change.

Some toys look like living things.

Some toys move like living things.

But they are nonliving.

Nonliving Things Around You

Toys are nonliving things.

Animals grow.

Animals change.

Animals can move.

Animals have babies.

What do plants need?

Plants need air.
Plants need water.

They do not need food.
They do not need water.
They do not grow on their own.

Plants need Sun.

Plants need space to grow.

What are nonliving things?

Nonliving things were never alive.

What do animals need?

Animals need food.

Animals need water.

Animals need air.

Animals need space to live.

Animals need shelter.

A **shelter** is a safe place.

Habitats

by Arlene Block

Genre	Comprehension Skill	Text Features	Science Content
Nonfiction	Picture Clues	• Labels • Glossary	Habitats

Scott Foresman Science 1.2

PEARSON
Scott Foresman

DK

scottforesman.com

ISBN 0-328-13736-7

9 780328 137367   90000

What did you learn?

1. What do plants and animals get from their habitats?

2. How are a desert and an ocean alike? How are they different?

3. **Writing** in Science The forest changes in winter. Write to explain some of the changes. Use words from the book as you write.

4. **Picture Clues** Look at the pictures on page 5. Use picture clues to tell one animal that lives in the forest.

Photographs: Every effort has been made to secure permission and provide appropriate credit for photographic material. The publisher deeply regrets any omission and pledges to correct errors called to its attention in subsequent editions. Unless otherwise acknowledged, all photographs are the property of Scott Foresman, a division of Pearson Education. Photo locators denoted as follows: Top (T), Center (C), Bottom (B), Left (L), Right (R) Background (Bkgd) Opener: (Bkgd) Getty Images, (TR) Stephen Dalton/Photo Researchers, Inc.
Title Page: Getty Images 2 ©W. Perry Conway/Corbis 4 ©Jeffrey Lepore/Photo Researchers, Inc. 5 ©Daniel J. Cox/Natural Exposures 6 Getty Images 7 ©Daniel J. Cox/Natural Exposures 8 ©David Samuel Robbins/Corbis 9 (C, BL) Getty Images, (BC) ©Joe McDonald/Corbis 10 Digital Vision 11 (CR) ©Flip Nicklin/Minden Pictures, (B, C)Getty Images 12 (B) ©Yva Momatiuk/John Eastcott/ Minden Pictures 13 (B) ©Jose Fuste Raga/Corbis 14 (B) ©David Samuel Robbins/Corbis 15 (T) Digital Vision, (BL) ©Daniel J. Cox/Natural Exposures

ISBN: 0-328-13736-7

Copyright © Pearson Education, Inc.

All Rights Reserved. Printed in the United States of America. The blackline masters in this publication are designed for use with appropriate equipment to reproduce copies for classroom use only. Scott Foresman grants permission to classroom teachers to reproduce from these masters.

2 3 4 5 6 7 8 9 10 V004 13 12 11 10 09 08 07 06 05

Glossary

desert a habitat that is very dry

forest a habitat that has many trees

habitat a place where plants and animals live

ocean a habitat that has salt water

wetland a habitat that is covered with water

Habitats

by Arlene Block

What is a forest habitat?

Plants and animals live in a **habitat.**
A habitat gives shelter.
A habitat has what they need.

Animals live in many habitats.
Plants and animals get what they
need in their habitats.

Plants live in many habitats.

A **forest** is a habitat.

Animals live in a forest.

A forest has trees and plants.

Forest Plants and Animals

It is summer.

Animals can get food.

Animals can get water.

Plants and animals live in a desert.

This animal lives in a desert.

It needs very little water.

What is a desert habitat?

A **desert** is a habitat.

A desert is very dry.

A desert gets a lot of sun.

Plants can get sun.

Plants can get water.

It is winter.
How did the forest change?

Plants live in an ocean.
Animals live in an ocean.
An ocean has what they need.

Sea turtle

Whale

Fish

What is an ocean habitat?

An **ocean** is a habitat.

An ocean has salt water.

Plants get less sun.

Some trees drop their leaves.

It is hard for some animals to find food.

What is a wetland habitat?

A **wetland** is a habitat.

A wetland is covered with water.

Animals live in a wetland.

Plants live in a wetland.

A wetland has what they need.

Crane

Frog

Dragonfly

How Plants and Animals Live

by Tristan F. Nicholas

Genre	Comprehension Skill	Text Features	Science Content
Nonfiction	Alike and Different	• Call Outs • Glossary	Animals and Plants

Scott Foresman Science 1.3

What did you learn?

1. What parts of a bird help it get food?

2. How does a stem help a plant?

3. **Writing** in Science Camouflage helps some living things stay safe. Write to explain how one living thing in the book uses camouflage to stay safe. Use words from the book as you write.

4. **Alike and Different** How are the ways animals and plants stay safe alike? How are the ways animals and plants stay safe different?

Photographs: Every effort has been made to secure permission and provide appropriate credit for photographic material. The publisher deeply regrets any omission and pledges to correct errors called to its attention in subsequent editions. Unless otherwise acknowledged, all photographs are the property of Scott Foresman, a division of Pearson Education. Photo locators denoted as follows: Top (T), Center (C), Bottom (B), Left (L), Right (R) Background (Bkgd)
Opener: (Bkgd) ©Michael Patrick O'Neill/NHPA Limited, (TL) ©DK Images
Title Page: ©DK Images; 2 ©Taxi/Getty Images; 3 ©DK Images; 4 ©Noboru Komine/Photo Researchers, Inc.; 5 ©S. Purdy Matthews/Stone/Getty Images; 6 (CC) T. Kitchin and V. Hurst/NHPA Limited,(B) ©DK Images, (T) Stephen Krasemann/Stone; 7 Dante Fenolio/Photo Researchers, Inc.; 8 ©Virginia Neetus/Animals Animals/Earth Sciences; 9 © Chase Swift/Corbis; 12 ©DK Images; 13 (CL, CR) ©DK Images, (BC) ©John Eastcott and Yva Momatiuk/NGS Image Collection; 14 ©DK Images; 15 ©DK Images

ISBN: 0-328-13739-1

How Plants and
Animals Live

by Tristan F. Nicholas

Glossary

antennae — feelers that help animals feel, smell, and taste

camouflage — a color or shape that makes a living thing hard to see

flower — the part of the plant that makes seeds

leaf — the part of the plant that makes food

root — the part of the plant that takes in water and holds the plant in the ground

stem — the part of the plant that moves water to other parts

What helps animals live in their habitats?

Animals live in many habitats.
Their body parts help them.
Some animals live in cold habitats.
Fur helps them keep warm.

Plants and animals live in many habitats.
Plants and animals use their parts to help them live.
Plants and animals help each other.

What helps protect plants?

Spines keep animals away.

Spines help some plants stay safe.

Some plants use camouflage.

Camouflage makes the plants hard

to see.

Living in the Ocean

Shells keep some animals safe.

Some animals have **antennae.**

Antennae are feelers.

Antennae help them smell and

taste too.

How do animals get food?

Animals use parts of their bodies
to get food.
Birds use beaks to eat food.
Camels store fat in their humps.
They use the fat for food.

Some plants have spines.
Some plants have needles.

Plants in Different Habitats

Plants grow in many habitats.

Some plants have leaves.

Leaves have many sizes.

Leaves have many shapes.

Other Ways Animals Get Food

Lions have strong legs.

Lions can run fast.

Lions can catch food.

What can help protect animals?

Camouflage makes an animal or plant hard to see.
Camouflage can be a color or a shape.
Camouflage helps living things stay safe.

The **leaf** makes food.
The **flower** makes seeds.
The **stem** moves water in the plant.

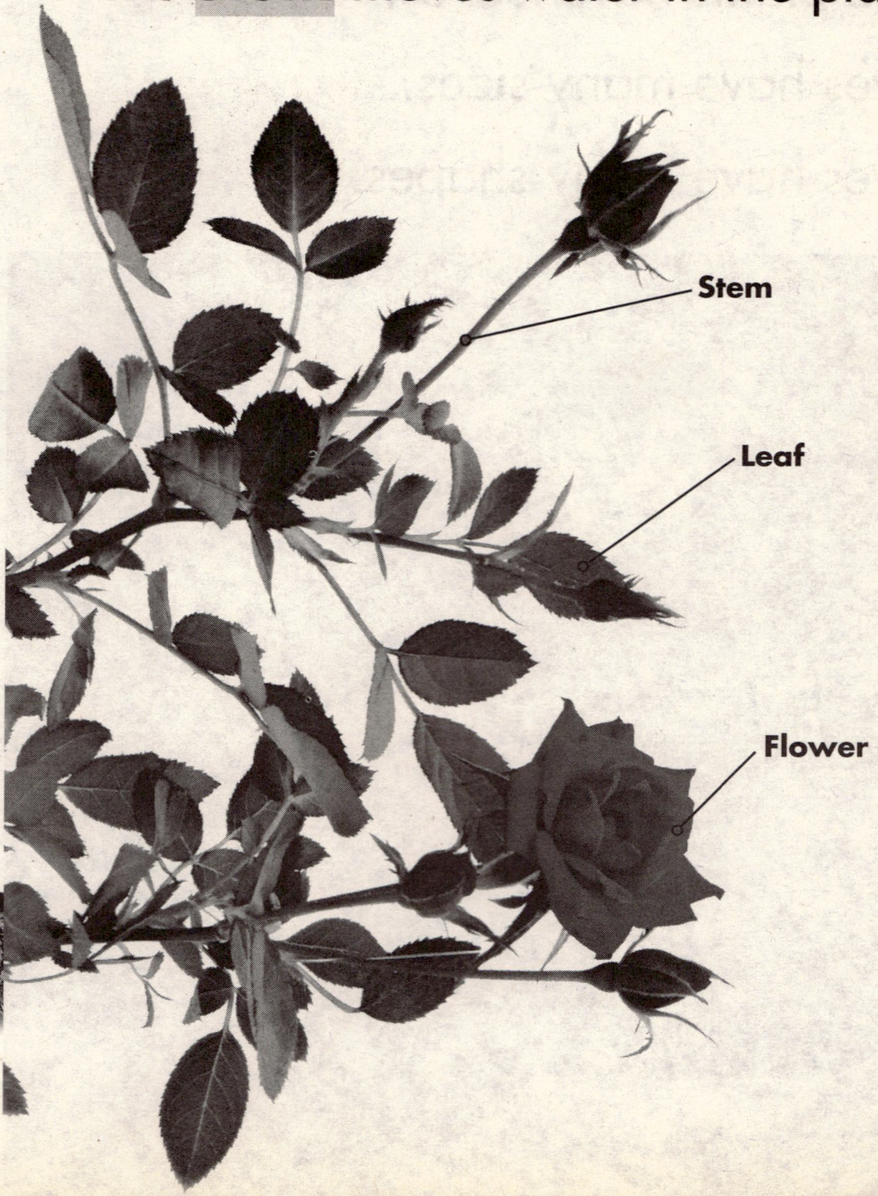

What are some parts of plants?

Plant parts help plants live.

Roots take in water.

Roots hold plants in the ground.

Hiding in the Water

The crocodile lives in the water.

It keeps its eyes above the water.

The other animals do not see it.

Animals Warn of Danger

Animals help each other stay safe.
A deer lifts its tail when it is
in danger.
Other deer can see the tail.
They run away to stay safe.

A peacock makes a loud call.
Other peacocks hide to stay safe.

Life Cycles

by Steven Danan

Genre	Comprehension Skill	Text Features	Science Content
Nonfiction	Put Things in Order	• Diagrams • Glossary	Life Cycles

Scott Foresman Science 1.4

PEARSON

Scott Foresman

scottforesman.com

ISBN 0-328-13742-1

9 780328 137428

90000

What did you learn?

1. How does a caterpillar change as it grows?

2. What is a tadpole?

3. **Writing** in Science Animals change as they grow. Write to explain how they can change. Use words from the book as you write.

4. ⟳ **Put Things in Order** Tell the steps in the life cycle of a daisy in order.

Photographs: Every effort has been made to secure permission and provide appropriate credit for photographic material. The publisher deeply regrets any omission and pledges to correct errors called to its attention in subsequent editions. Unless otherwise acknowledged, all photographs are the property of Scott Foresman, a division of Pearson Education. Photo locators denoted as follows:
Top (T), Center (C), Bottom (B), Left (L), Right (R) Background (Bkgd)
Opener: ©Allen Russell/Index Stock Imagery Title Page: ©DK Images 2 (CL, BR) © DK Images 3 ©DK Images 4 ©DK Images 5 (CL, BC, CR) ©DK Images 6 (CL) ©George D. Lepp/Corbis, (BC) ©Michael and Patricia Fogden/Corbis, (CR) ©DK Images 7 ©George D. Lepp/Corbis 8 (B) ©Joseph T. Collins/ Photo Researchers, Inc., (CR) ©T. Wiewandt/DRK Photo 9 ©Pam Francis/Getty Images, ©Pat Doyle/ Corbis 11 ©DK Images 12 ©David Young-Wolff/Photo Edit 13 ©DK Images, (R) ©Bill Ross/Corbis 14 (CL) ©DK Images, (BL) Brand X Pictures 15 ©Allen Russell/Index Stock Imagery

ISBN: 0-328-13742-1

Copyright © Pearson Education, Inc.

All Rights Reserved. Printed in the United States of America. The blackline masters in this publication are designed for use with appropriate equipment to reproduce copies for classroom use only. Scott Foresman grants permission to classroom teachers to reproduce from these masters.

2 3 4 5 6 7 8 9 10 V004 13 12 11 10 09 08 07 06 05

Life Cycles

by Steven Danan

Glossary

larva   a young insect

life cycle   all the changes of a living thing as it grows

pupa   what the larva may become as it changes into a grown insect

seed coat   a hard cover that protects a seed

seedling   a young plant

tadpole   a young frog

33

How does a frog grow?

A frog starts as an egg.
A tadpole swims out of the egg.
A **tadpole** is a young frog.

Plants and animals have life cycles.
Plants and animals grow and change.

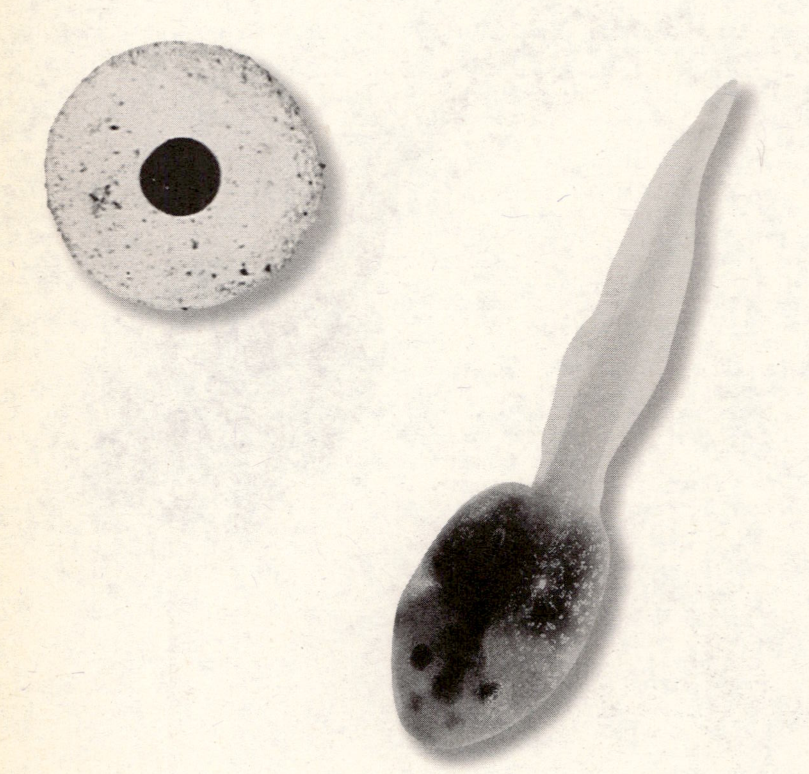

How do plants grow and change?

Flowers have different colors.

Flowers have different shapes.

Flowers have different patterns.

Plants can change as they grow.

The tadpole has a tail.

The tadpole lives in water.

The tadpole grows and changes.

Grown Frog

The tadpole grows into a frog.

The frog lives in water.

The frog lives on land too.

How a Cherry Tree Grows

A cherry tree grows fruit.

Cherry trees make cherries.

Cherry trees grow from cherry seeds.

How does a tree grow?

Trees grow from seeds.

Trees change as they grow.

Trees take many years to grow.

Tadpoles become frogs.

They grow and change.

These changes are called a

life cycle.

How does a butterfly grow?

A butterfly starts as an egg.
A larva comes out of the egg.
A butterfly larva is a caterpillar.
A **larva** is a young insect.

A daisy starts as a seed.
Roots, a stem, and flowers grow.
Flowers make seeds.
This is the life cycle of a daisy.

How does a daisy grow?

Most plants grow from seeds.

A **seed coat** covers the seed.

It keeps the seed safe.

A seedling grows from the seed.

The **seedling** is a young plant.

The caterpillar grows.

It makes a hard cover.

It is called a **pupa** as it changes in the cover.

It comes out as a butterfly.

How do animals grow and change?

Young animals change as they grow.

They can change size.

They can change shape.

They can change color.

Growing Up

Young animals grow up.

They can look like their parents.

They can also look different.

Food Chains

by Rose Murray

Genre	Comprehension Skill	Text Features	Science Content
Nonfiction	Draw Conclusions	• Diagrams • Labels • Glossary	Food Chains

Scott Foresman Science 1.5

PEARSON
Scott Foresman

DK

ISBN 0-328-13745-6

90000

9 780328 137459

scottforesman.com

Vocabulary

food chain

marsh

oxygen

rain forest

What did you learn?

1. What do animals eat?

2. How does water move in a plant?

3. **Writing** in Science Plants and animals are linked in food chains. Write to explain how a food chain works. Use words from the book as you write.

4. **Draw Conclusions** What would a green plant be unable to do if it loses its leaves?

Food Chains

by Rose Murray

Glossary

food chain — the connection between living things and their food

marsh — a wetland habitat

oxygen — a gas in the air

rain forest — a habitat that gets lots of rain

How do plants and animals get food?

All living things have needs.

All living things need food.

Food chains are in all kinds of places.

All living things are linked in food chains.

Some animals eat plants.

Some animals eat other animals.

Some animals eat plants and other animals.

Finding Food

Animals find other animals to eat.

A bird can catch a snake.

The snake is food for the bird.

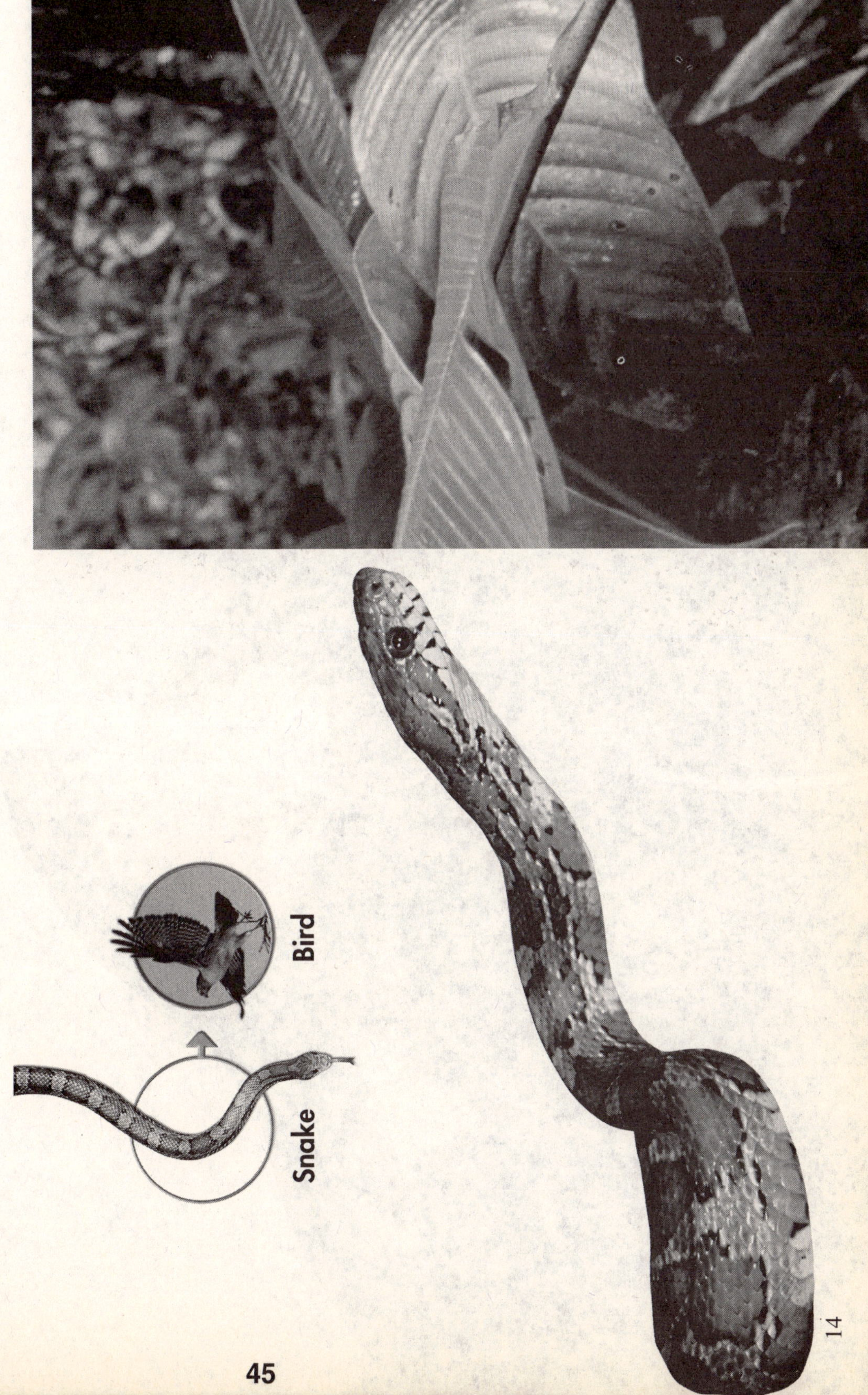

45

Plants Make Food

Plants need food.

Green leaves make food for a plant.

Leaves use three things to make food.

Plants in marshes make food.

They use light from the Sun.

Animals eat these plants.

Other animals eat these animals.

How do living things
get food in a marsh?

A **marsh** is a wetland habitat.

It is a wet place.

Marshes have food chains too.

Leaves use air.

Leaves use water.

Leaves use light from the Sun.

Roots take in water from soil.
The water goes up the stem
to the leaves.

Plants make food.
Animals eat plants.
Other animals eat these animals.
This is called a **food chain.**

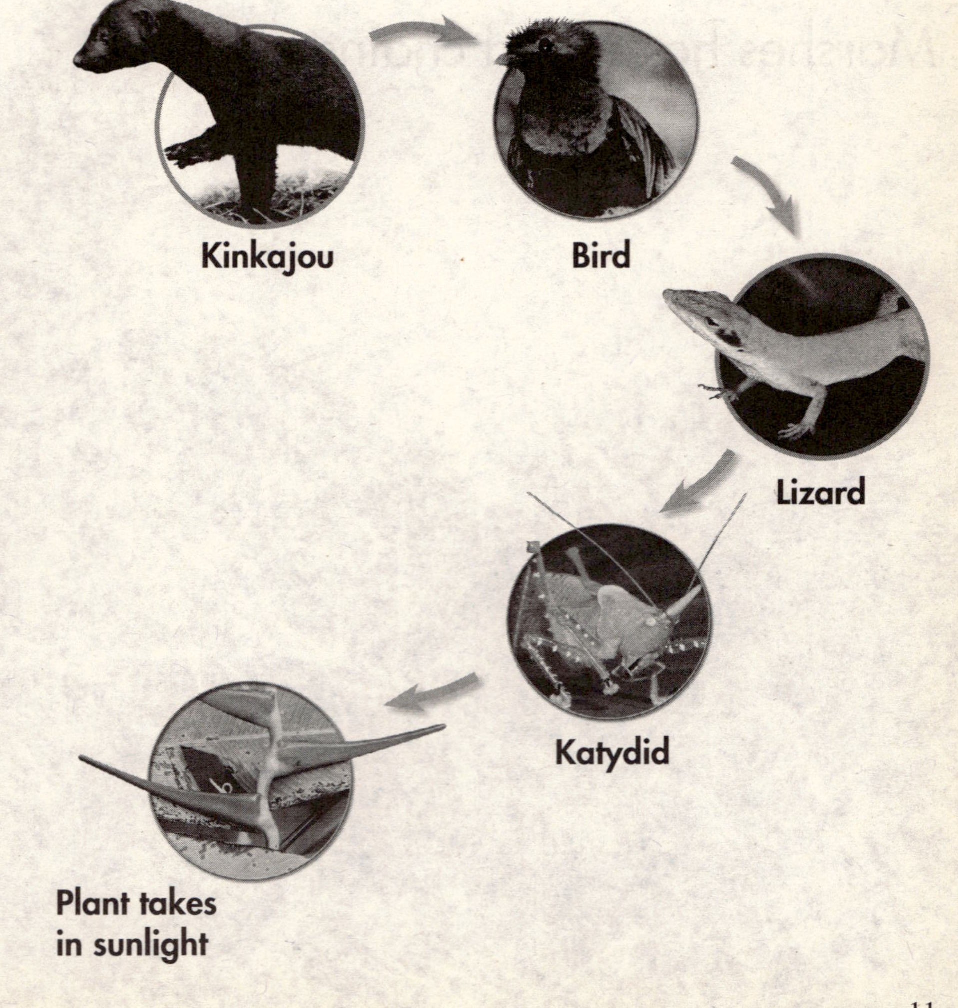

48

Food for Animals

Some animals find other
animals to eat.
This is their food.

Green leaves give off oxygen when
they make food.
Oxygen is a gas in the air.
Plants and animals need oxygen
to live.

How do living things get food in a rain forest?

A **rain forest** is a habitat.

A rain forest gets lots of rain.

A plant grows in the rain forest.

The plant makes its own food.

An animal eats the plant.

Another animal eats this animal.

Land, Water, and Air

by Leslie Rotsky

Genre	Comprehension Skill	Text Features	Science Content
Nonfiction	Important Details	• Labels • Glossary	Natural Resources

Scott Foresman Science 1.6

PEARSON
Scott Foresman

scottforesman.com

ISBN 0-328-13748-0

90000

9 780328 137480

51

Vocabulary

clay	natural resource
erosion	rocks
humus	sand
minerals	weathering

What did you learn?

1. Is there more water or land on Earth?

2. What is a natural resource?

3. **Writing** in Science Weathering and erosion are two things that can change rocks. Write to explain the ways rocks can change. Use words from the book as you write.

4. **Important Details** How do plants help slow down erosion?

Photographs: Every effort has been made to secure permission and provide appropriate credit for photographic material. The publisher deeply regrets any omission and pledges to correct errors called to its attention in subsequent editions. Unless otherwise acknowledged, all photographs are the property of Scott Foresman, a division of Pearson Education. Photo locators denoted as follows:
Top (T), Center (C), Bottom (B), Left (L), Right (R) Background (Bkgd)
Opener: (Bkgd) ©Steve Raymer/NGS Image Collection, (BR) ©Paul Chesley/NGS Image Collection; Title Page: ©Steve Dunwell/Getty Images; 2 (CC) ©Thomas Kitchin/Tom Stack & Associates, Inc., (B) ©Richard Price/Getty Images; 3 (BL) ©Craig Aurness/Corbis, (CL) Silver Burdett Ginn, (CR) ©J. Jangoux/Photo Researchers, Inc., (BC) ©James Havey/Index Stock Imagery; 4 ©J. Eastcott Film/NGS Image Collection; 5 (T) ©Galen Rowell/Corbis, (B) ©W. Perry Conway/Corbis; 6 (CL) ©Getty Images, (CL) ©J. P. Ferrero/Jacana/Photo Researchers, Inc.; 7 (B) ©DK Images, (CR) ©Barry L. Runk/Grant Heilman Photography; 8 (BL) ©Garry D. McMichael/Photo Researchers, Inc., (CC) ©Michael Marten/Photo Researchers, Inc.; 9 ©Barry L. Runk/Grant Heilman Photography; 10 (BC) ©Image Source Limited; 11 ©Cosmo Condina/Getty Images; 12 (CC) ©Royalty-Free/Corbis, (BC) ©Michael T. Sedam/Corbis; 13 ©DK Images

ISBN: 0-328-13748-0

Copyright © Pearson Education, Inc.

Glossary

clay	a sticky, soft part of soil
erosion	when wind or water moves rocks and soil
humus	a part of soil made of parts of living things that died
minerals	nonliving things found in rocks and soil
natural resource	a useful thing that comes from nature
rocks	nonliving things that come from Earth
sand	tiny pieces of broken rock
weathering	when rocks break apart and change

Land, Water, and Air
by Leslie Rotsky

What makes up Earth?

Land and water cover the Earth.
There is more water than land.
Earth has different kinds of land.
Earth has different kinds of water.

Living things use natural resources.
Natural resources come from Earth.
We need the land, air, and water
of Earth.

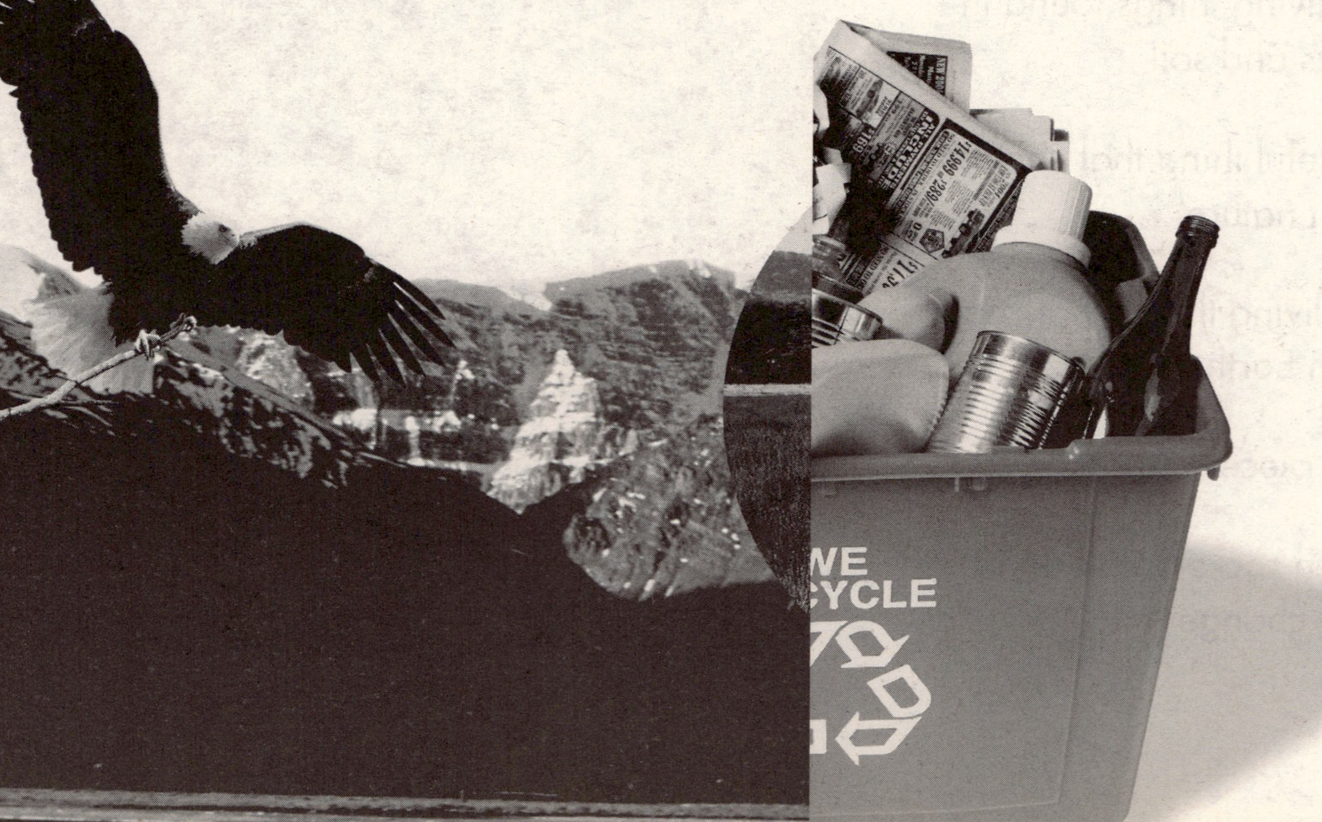

How can you reduce, reuse, and recycle?

Help save land, water, and air.

Reduce how much you use.

Reuse things again and again.

Recycle old things into new things.

Kinds of Land and Water

A plain is flat land.

A hill is land that gets higher.

A lake is water with land all around it.

A river is water that flows through land.

River

Plain

Lake

What are rocks and soil?

Rocks are nonliving things.

Rocks can be many colors, sizes, and shapes.

Big rocks are called boulders.

Sand is tiny pieces of broken rock.

Minerals come from the land.

Minerals are in rocks and soil.

Copper is a mineral.

People use copper to make pennies.

Using Land

Land is a natural resource.

People grow food on land.

Trees grow on land.

People use wood to build things.

Rocks are a natural resource.

They come from Earth.

A **natural resource** is a part of Earth.

A natural resource is a useful thing.

Soil

Soil is a natural resource.

Soil can be made of sand, clay, and humus.

Sand is rough and loose.

Clay is sticky and soft.

Humus is made of parts of living things that died.

Sand

Clay

Humus

Using Water

Living things use water.

Water is a natural resource.

How do living things use natural resources?

Air is a natural resource.

Plants and trees need air.

Some animals fly in the air.

People and animals breathe air.

Worms help make soil loose.

Loose soil helps plants grow.

Humus in soil helps plants grow.

What changes land?

Weathering is when rocks break and change.
Wind, water, and ice cause weathering.
It can change the size, shape, and color of rocks.

Erosion can change land too.
Erosion is when rocks and soil move.
Wind or water causes erosion.
Plant roots hold soil in place.
This can slow down erosion.

Weather

by Judy Healy

61

Genre	Comprehension Skill	Text Features	Science Content
Nonfiction	Predict	• Captions • Glossary	Weather

Scott Foresman Science 1.7

PEARSON
Scott Foresman

scottforesman.com

ISBN 0-328-13751-0

90000

9 780328 137510

What did you learn?

1. What tool can you use to measure the temperature?

2. What are two kinds of wet weather?

3. **Writing** in Science Seasons come in a pattern. Write to name the four seasons and to describe the order in which they happen. Use words from the book as you write.

4. **Predict** It is raining. The air gets cold. What will happen to the rain?

Photographs: Every effort has been made to secure permission and provide appropriate credit for photographic material. The publisher deeply regrets any omission and pledges to correct errors called to its attention in subsequent editions. Unless otherwise acknowledged, all photographs are the property of Scott Foresman, a division of Pearson Education. Photo locators denoted as follows: Top (T), Center (C), Bottom (B), Left (L), Right (R) Background (Bkgd)
Opener: ©Taxi/Getty Images; Title Page: ©Zefa Visual Media/Index Stock Imagery; 2 ©Marc Muench/Corbis; 3 ©Paul A. Souders/Corbis; 4 (BL) ©Nigel J. Dennis/Gallo Images/Corbis, (BR) ©Marc Muench/Corbis; 5 (BL) ©Bruce Peebles/Corbis, (BR) ©Taxi/Getty Images, (L) ©Stone/Getty Images; 6 ©Stone/Getty Images; 7 ©John Mead/Photo Researchers, Inc.; 8 ©Maslowski Photo/Photo Researchers, Inc.; 9 ©Stone/Getty Images; 10 ©David Pollack/Corbis; 11 ©Stone/Getty Images; 13 (TL, TR, BL, BR) ©Taxi/Getty Images; 14 (C) ©Stephen Oliver/©DK Images, (CC) Matthew Ward/©DK Images, (BR) ©Everett Johnson/Index Stock Imagery; 15 ©Zefa Visual Media/Index Stock Imagery

ISBN: 0-328-13751-0

Copyright © Pearson Education, Inc.

All Rights Reserved. Printed in the United States of America. The blackline masters in this publication are designed for use with appropriate equipment to reproduce copies for classroom use only. Scott Foresman grants permission to classroom teachers to reproduce from these masters.

2 3 4 5 6 7 8 9 10 V004 13 12 11 10 09 08 07 06 05

Glossary

clouds	many tiny drops of water or ice
season	a time of year
sleet	frozen rain
temperature	how hot or cold something is
thermometer	a tool used to measure temperature
water vapor	a form of water in the air
weather	what it is like outside

Weather

by Judy Healy

How can you measure weather?

Weather is what it is like outside.
Weather changes.

There are all kinds of weather.
How is the weather today where you live?

After winter is spring again.

Seasons always come and

go in this way.

This is a pattern.

It can be windy.

It can be still.

It can be wet or dry.

There can be clouds or Sun.

Temperature is how hot
or cold something is.
A **thermometer** is a tool to
measure temperature.

After spring is summer.

Spring is warm.

Summer is warmer.

After summer is fall.

After fall is winter.

Fall is cooler and winter is coldest.

Fall

Winter

What are the four seasons?

A **season** is a time of year.

There are four seasons.

The seasons are spring, summer, fall, and winter.

A wind vane tells which way wind blows.

A rain gauge tells how much rain falls.

How do clouds form?

Water is in the air all the time.
Water vapor is water in the air.

We cannot see water vapor.

In a blizzard there is lots of snow.

The wind blows hard!

Some animals have fur to stay warm.

Snowy Weather

It gets cold.

Snow falls from clouds.

Snow is frozen water in the air.

Water vapor cools.

Clouds form.

Clouds can be different shapes.

Clouds can be different sizes.

Tiny drops of water make up **clouds.**

What are some kinds of wet weather?

Rain is wet weather.
Plants need rainwater to live.
Some living things want to stay
dry in rain.

Rain can change if it is cold.
Rain can turn into sleet.
Sleet is frozen rain.
Sleet is wet weather too.

Observing Matter

by Anna Schlecker

Genre	Comprehension Skill	Text Feature	Science Content
Nonfiction	Alike and Different	• Glossary	Matter

Scott Foresman Science 1.8

PEARSON
Scott Foresman

DK

ISBN 0-328-13754-5

90000

9 780328 137541

scottforesman.com

What did you learn?

1. What are some things in your classroom that are made of matter?

2. How can you describe matter?

3. **Writing** in Science Matter can change. Write to describe one way matter can change. Use words from the book as you write.

4. **Alike and Different** How is a solid like a liquid? How is it different?

Illustration: 2 David Preiss
Photographs: Every effort has been made to secure permission and provide appropriate credit for photographic material. The publisher deeply regrets any omission and pledges to correct errors called to its attention in subsequent editions. Unless otherwise acknowledged, all photographs are the property of Scott Foresman, a division of Pearson Education. Photo locators denoted as follows:
Top (T), Center (C), Bottom (B), Left (L), Right (R) Background (Bkgd)
Opener: ©Rob Lewine/Corbis; 3 ©Rob Lewine/Corbis; 4 (BC) ©DK Images; 5 (CC) ©DK Images

ISBN: 0-328-13754-5

Observing Matter

by Anna Schlecker

Glossary

dissolve	to spread throughout a liquid
evaporate	to change from a liquid to a gas
gas	matter that can change size and shape
liquid	matter that takes the shape of its container
mass	the amount of matter in an object
matter	anything that takes up space
solid	matter that takes up space and has its own shape

What is matter?

Matter takes up space.

It has **mass.**

It has tiny parts.

Some parts are too small to see.

Paper is a solid.

Paper can burn.

It will not turn back into paper.

Matter is all around us.

It can change.

What are other ways matter changes?

Heat makes water evaporate.

Evaporate means to change from liquid to gas.

The Sun can make water on the ground evaporate.

Describing Matter

Matter can have different shapes.

It can have different sizes.

How are the things in this picture alike and different?

What are solids, liquids, and gases?

A **solid** is matter.

It takes up space.

A solid does not change shape.

Heat melts ice.

The ice changes to water.

Water boils when it gets very hot.

The water changes to a gas.

This gas is water vapor.

How can water change?

Water is a liquid.

Water can freeze when it gets cold.

The water changes to ice.

Ice is a solid.

A **liquid** is matter.

A liquid is in this bottle.

It takes the shape of the bottle.

A liquid takes the shape of what

it is in.

A **gas** is matter.

It takes up space.

It can change size and shape.

It takes the shape of what it is in.

Some solids dissolve in liquids.

Dissolve means to spread
throughout a liquid.

Mixing Solids and Liquids

Soup is made of solids and liquids.

The solids and liquids are mixed.

You can take the solids out of the liquid.

Bubbles are filled with air.

Air is a gas.

How does matter change?

Matter can change.

It can change in many ways.

A liquid can freeze when it is cold.

A solid can melt when it is hot.

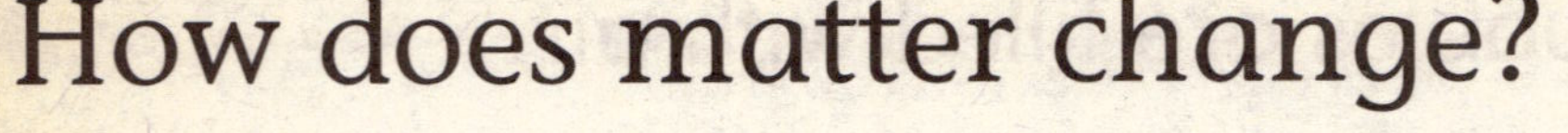

Movement and Sound

by Heidi Gillis

Genre	Comprehension Skill	Text Features	Science Content
Nonfiction	Cause and Effect	• Captions • Glossary	Forces and Sound

Scott Foresman Science 1.9

PEARSON
Scott Foresman

DK

ISBN 0-328-13757-X

9 780328 137572

90000

scottforesman.com

What did you learn?

1. What kind of force makes things fall to the ground?

2. How can you make a toy car go fast?

3. **Writing** in Science Magnets have poles. Write to explain how the poles of magnets work. Use words from the book as you write.

4. **Cause and Effect** You have two toys. One is a metal car and one is a rubber duck. A magnet attracts the car but not the duck. Why?

Photographs: Every effort has been made to secure permission and provide appropriate credit for photographic material. The publisher deeply regrets any omission and pledges to correct errors called to its attention in subsequent editions. Unless otherwise acknowledged, all photographs are the property of Scott Foresman, a division of Pearson Education. Photo locators denoted as follows:
Top (T), Center (C), Bottom (B), Left (L), Right (R) Background (Bkgd)
Opener: ©Photographer's Choice/Getty Images; 2 ©Photodisc Green/Getty Images; 3 ©Frank Siteman/PhotoEdit; 4 Getty Images; 8 ©DK Images; 9 ©DK Images; 12 ©DK Images; 13 (TL) Getty Images, (BL) ©DK Images; 14 ©Alan Schein Photography/Corbis; 15 ©George F. Mobley/NGS Image Collection

ISBN: 0-328-13757-X

Movement and Sound

by Heidi Gillis

Glossary

attract   to pull toward

force   a push or a pull that may make something move

gravity   a force that pulls things toward the ground

magnet   an object that attracts some metal things

pole   at the end of some magnets

repel   to push away

speed   how quickly or slowly something moves

vibrate   to move back and forth very fast

What makes things move?

Force is a push or pull.

Force may make something move.

Push the sled up a hill.

Sounds of Nature

Sounds are all around.

Nature has sounds too.

What are ocean sounds?

What sounds are around us?

Many things make sounds.

Sounds can be loud or soft.

You can hear sounds on the street.

Gravity is a force.

Gravity pulls things down.

The sled goes down the hill.

The girl uses force to move the snow.

What is speed?

Push the car.

Push it with a lot of force.

It goes fast.

Speed is how fast or slow things move.

Tap the drum.

It makes a soft sound.

Hit the drum hard.

It makes a loud sound.

How are sounds made?

When a sound is made something vibrates.

Vibrate means to move back and forth very fast.

Push the car again.

Use less force.

Now the speed of the car is slow.

Force changes how things move.

How do things move?

Things can move up and down.
Things can move left and right.
They can go straight or curve.
How else can things move?

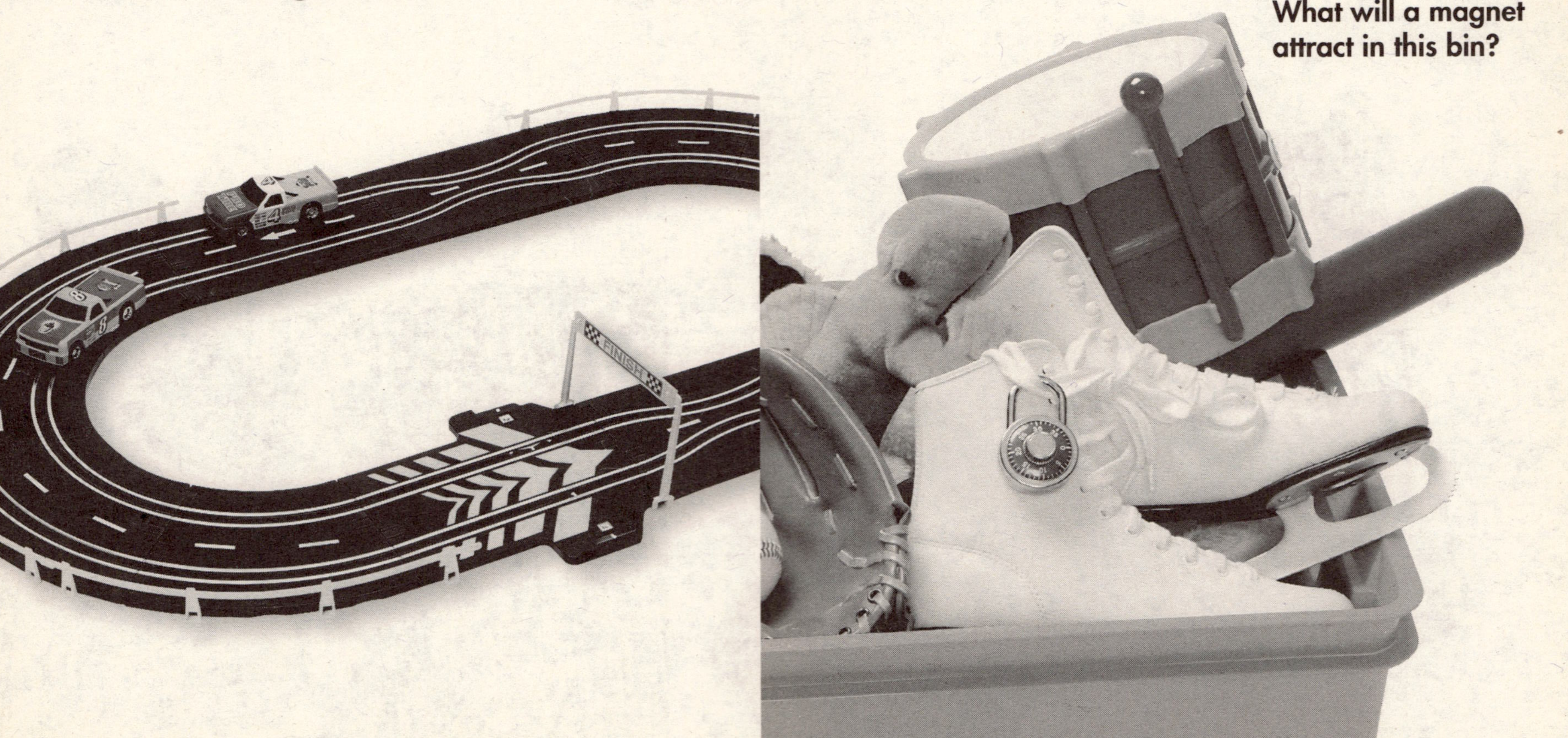

The magnet pulls more when it is
close to something.
It pulls less when it is far away.

Pulling Metal

Iron is a kind of metal.
Magnets attract things
made of iron.

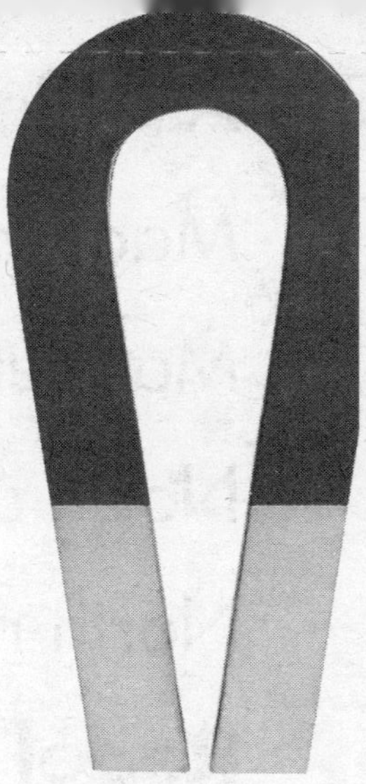

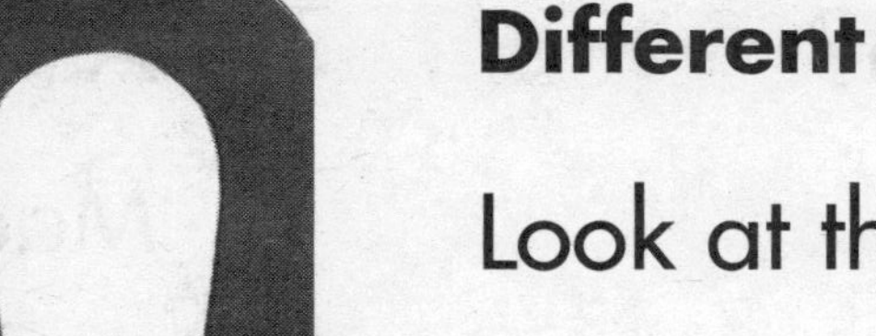

Different Places

Look at the blocks.
Which one is on top?
Which one is on the bottom?
Which one is next to the tower?

7

What do magnets do?

Look at the cars.

The ends of the cars are magnets.

A **magnet** attracts some metals.

Attract means to pull toward.

A **pole** is the end of some magnets.

Magnets have a north pole.

Magnets have a south pole.

North attracts south.

North repels north.

Repel means to push away.

Learning About Energy

by Tristan F. Nicholas

Genre	Comprehension Skill	Text Feature	Science Content
Nonfiction	Draw Conclusions	• Glossary	Energy

Scott Foresman Science 1.10

Vocabulary

battery

electricity

energy

fuel

heat

shadow

What did you learn?

1. What are some of the places light comes from?

2. What causes a shadow?

3. **Writing** in Science Shadows can change. Write to explain why shadows look different at different times of the day. Use words from the book as you write.

4. **Draw Conclusions** You flip a switch, but a lamp will not go on. It is not plugged in. Why won't it work?

Photographs: Every effort has been made to secure permission and provide appropriate credit for photographic material. The publisher deeply regrets any omission and pledges to correct errors called to its attention in subsequent editions. Unless otherwise acknowledged, all photographs are the property of Scott Foresman, a division of Pearson Education. Photo locators denoted as follows: Top (T), Center (C), Bottom (B), Left (L), Right (R) Background (Bkgd)
Opener: ©Tibor Bognár/Corbis; Title Page: ©Royalty-Free/Corbis; 2 ©Jose Fuste Raga/Corbis; 3 ©Ric Ergenbright/Corbis, ©Phil Degginger/Color-Pic, Inc.; 4 ©Royalty-Free/Corbis; 6 ©Royalty-Free/Corbis; 7 ©E. R. Degginger/Photo Researchers, Inc.; 9 Getty Images; 12 (BL) Getty Images; 13 Courtesy of the London Toy and Model Museum-Paddington, London/©DK Images; 14 ©Taxi/Getty Images

ISBN: 0-328-13760-X

Glossary

battery   something that stores energy

electricity   makes some things work

energy   can change things

fuel   anything that is burned to make heat or power

heat   moves from warmer places and objects to cooler places and objects

shadow   made when something blocks the light

Learning About Energy

by Tristan F. Nicholas

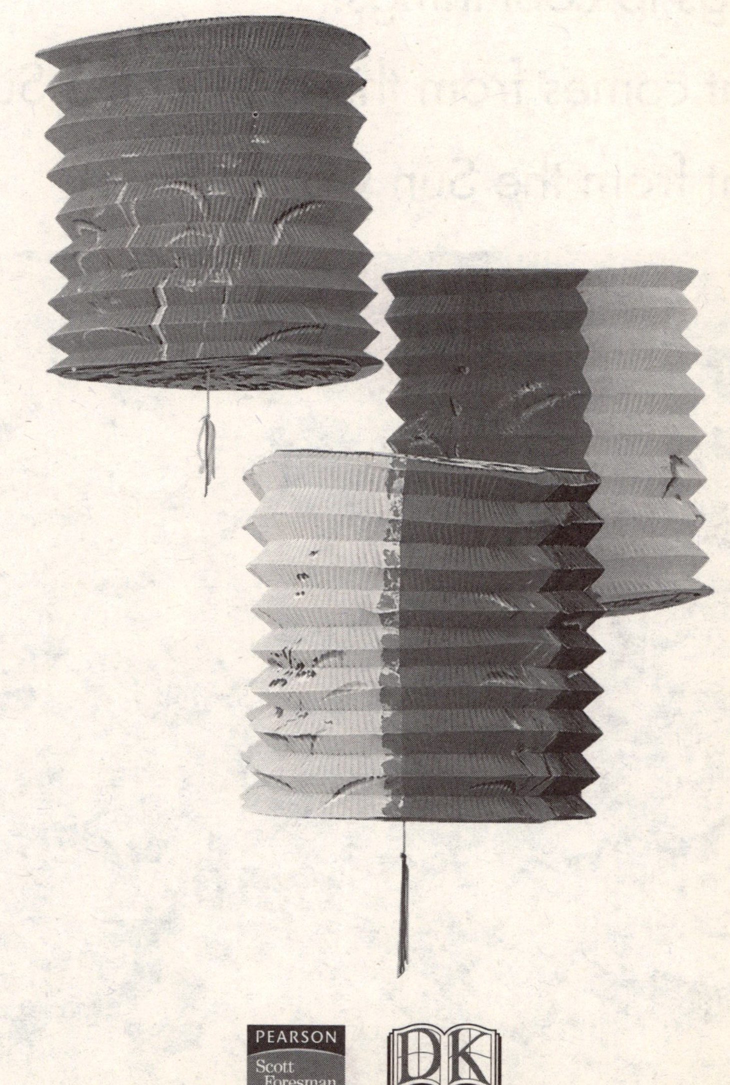

What gives off heat?

Heat moves from warm
things to cool things.
Heat comes from the light of the Sun.
Light from the Sun warms Earth.

How do you get energy?

You use energy all the time.
You get energy from food.
Energy helps you move and grow.

Using Energy

A fan gets energy from electricity.

Plug in the cord.

The toy gets energy from a battery.

A **battery** stores energy.

Heat

Heat comes from fire.

Heat makes things warm.

Heat comes from other things too.

What can energy do?

Light is a kind of energy.
Light from the Sun is energy.
Energy can change things.
It can change something from
cold to hot.

Electricity makes things
work.
Lights use electricity.

What uses energy around us?

Fuel is something that is burned.

It is burned to make heat or power.

Gasoline is a fuel.

A car burns gasoline.

Now the car has energy.

Dark colors take in a lot of light.

Light colors take in less light.

Things with light colors feel cooler.

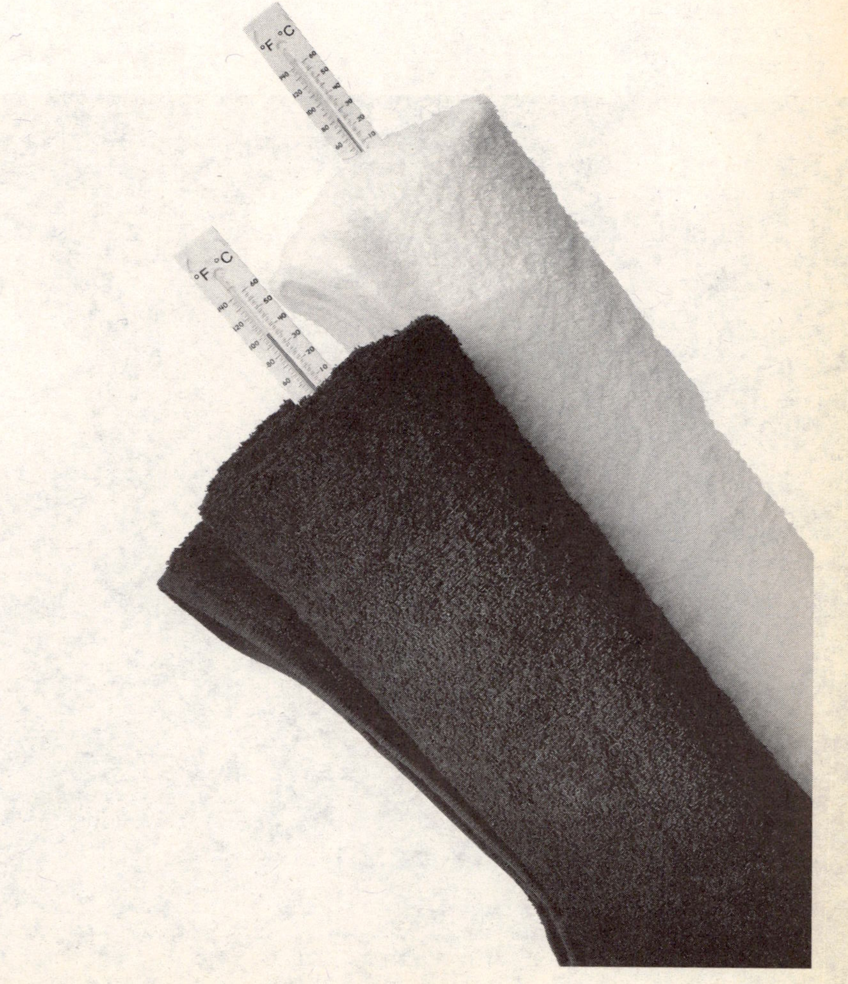

What makes light and shadows?

Light comes from the Sun.

Light comes from fire too.

The tree makes a different shadow at noon.

Shadows change when the Sun seems to move.

Changing Shadows

Shadows can change.

A tree makes a shadow in the morning.

Light comes from stars and candles.

Light even comes from this fly!

Where else does light come from?

Making Shadows

Things can block light.
Toys block light.
Shine the light
on the toy.
A shadow is made.

Shadows are made when things

block light.
The shadow is big when the light
is close.
The shadow is small when the light
is far away.

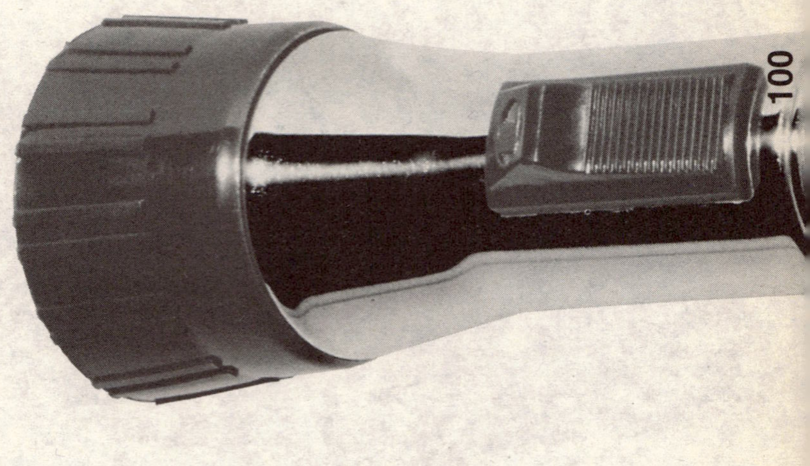

100

Day and Night Sky

by Rose Murray

Genre	Comprehension Skill	Text Features	Science Content
Nonfiction	Important Details	• Captions • Glossary	Day and Night Sky

Scott Foresman Science 1.11

Vocabulary

Moon

planet

rotation

star

Sun

telescope

What did you learn?

1. What do living things need from the Sun?

2. What movement of Earth makes day and night?

3. **Writing** in Science Many objects in the sky look small but they are not small. They are big. Write to explain this. Use words from the book as you write.

4. **Important Details** What words can you use to describe the Moon?

Illustrations: 6 Hank Dawson
Photographs: Every effort has been made to secure permission and provide appropriate credit for photographic material. The publisher deeply regrets any omission and pledges to correct errors called to its attention in subsequent editions. Unless otherwise acknowledged, all photographs are the property of Scott Foresman, a division of Pearson Education. Photo locators denoted as follows:
Top (T), Center (C), Bottom (B), Left (L), Right (R) Background (Bkgd)
Opener: ©Dale C. Spartas/Corbis; Title Page: ©Jet Propulsion Laboratory/NASA; 2 ©Dale C. Spartas/Corbis; 4 NASA; 5 (B) ©John Henley/Corbis, (C) ©Richard Glover/Corbis; 7 (C) ©Royalty-Free/Corbis, (B) ©Tibor Bognár/Corbis; 8 ©Roger Ressmeyer/Corbis; 9 ©Jerry Lodriguss/Photo Researchers, Inc.; 10 ©DK Images; 11 ©Roger Ressmeyer/Corbis; 12 ©Jet Propulsion Laboratory/NASA; 13 ©Johnson Space Center/NASA; 14 (CL, CCL, CCR) ©Dennis di Cicco/Corbis, (CR) ©Jeff Vanuga/Corbis; 15 ©Stone/Getty Images

ISBN: 0-328-13763-4

Glossary

Moon   an object that moves around Earth

planet   an object in the sky that does not give off light

rotation   Earth turning around and around

star   a big ball of hot gas

Sun   a big ball of hot gas that gives Earth light

telescope   a tool that makes things that are far away look closer

Day and Night Sky

by Rose Murray

What is in the day sky?

The **Sun** is a big ball of hot gas.
Light from the Sun warms Earth.
The Sun makes the day bright.
What can you see in the day sky?

Look at the sky in the day.
Look at the sky at night.
How are they different?
What can you see in the sky?

The Sun shines light on the Moon.

We only see the part that is lit.

The Moon looks different each night.

It looks the same again in about

29 days.

You may see clouds.

You may see the Moon too.

You can see the Moon more at night.

The Bright Sun

The Sun lights Earth.
This light keeps Earth warm.
Living things need this light.

The Moon is not like Earth.
It has no air.
It has no living things.

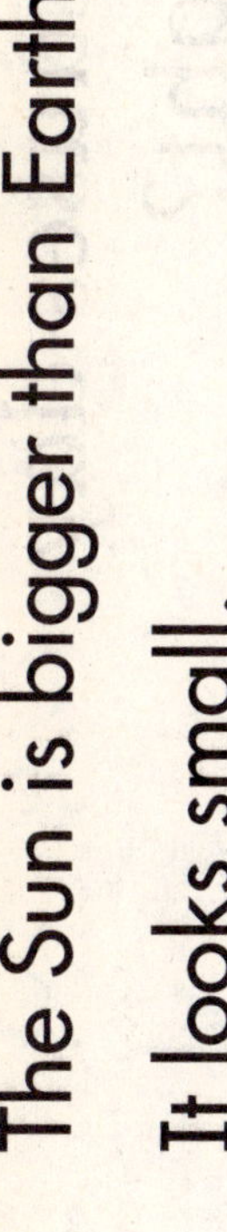

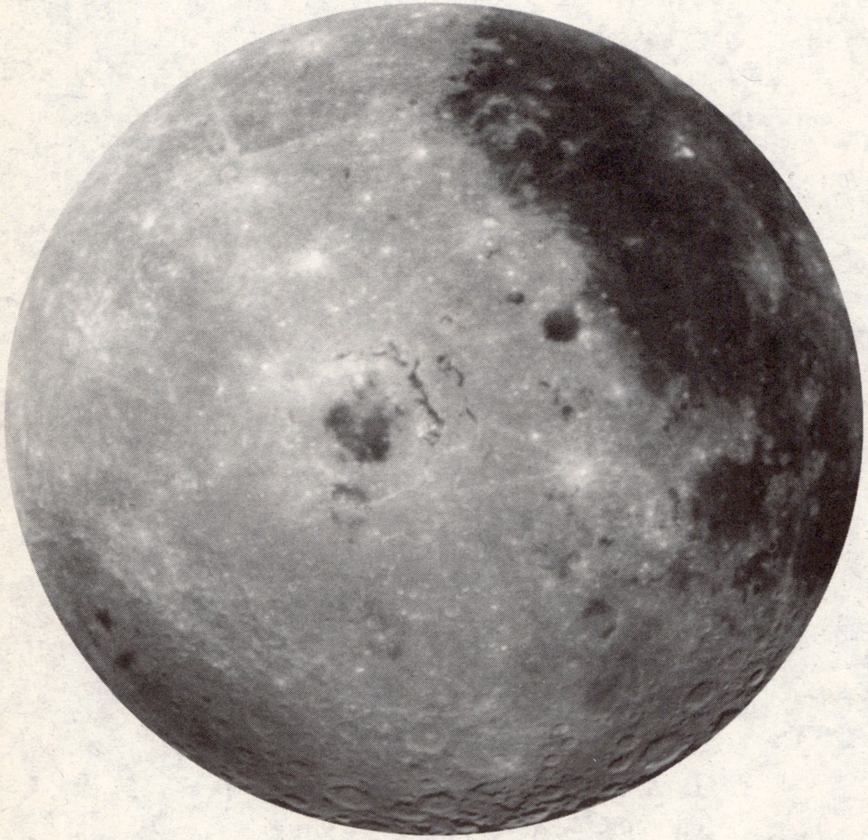

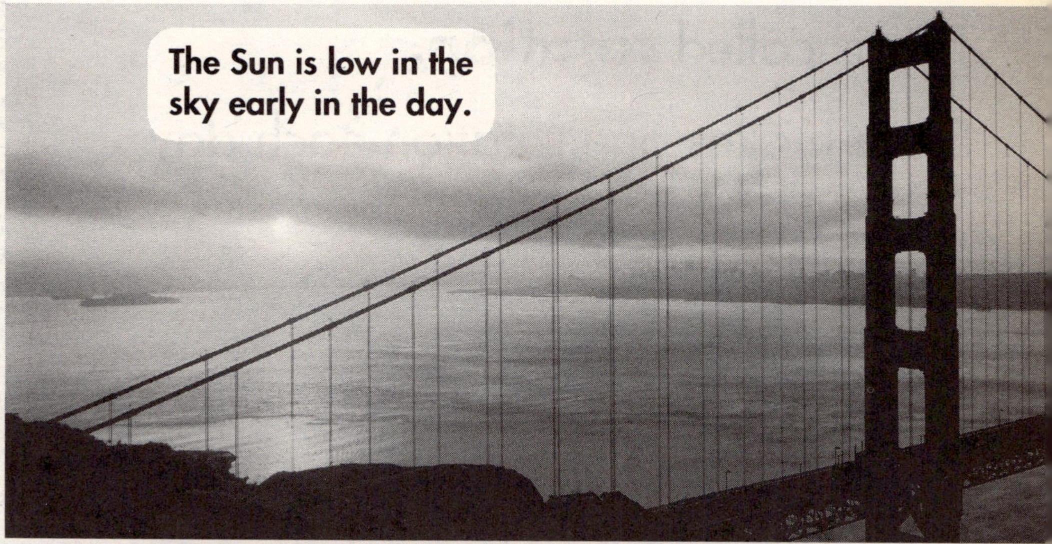

The Moon at Night

The **Moon** moves around Earth.

The Moon is round.

The Moon looks small.

It is far away.

The Sun is bigger than Earth.

It looks small.

It is far away.

It seems to move across the sky.

The Sun is low in the sky early in the day.

The Sun is above you at noon.

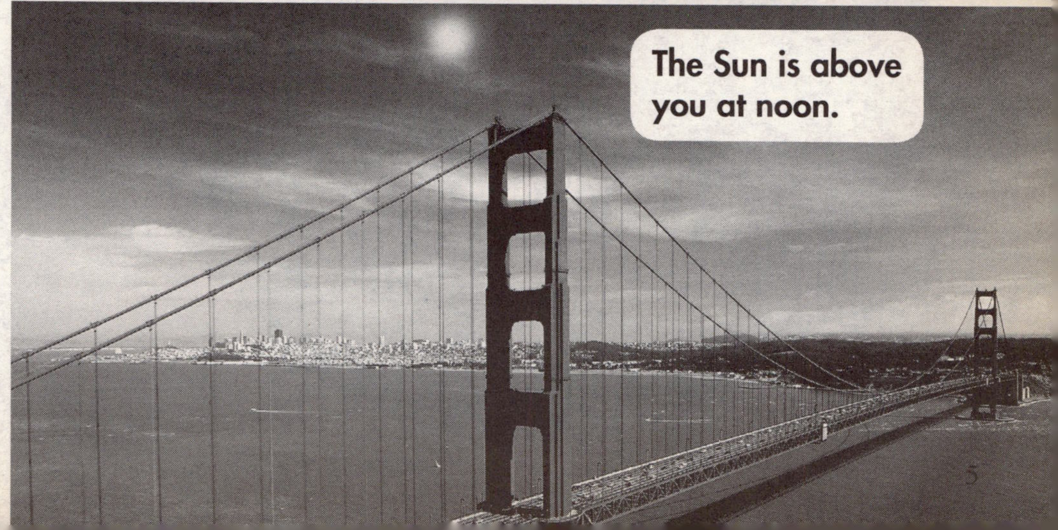

What causes day and night?

Earth is always moving.
Earth turns around and around.
This is called **rotation.**
Earth makes one rotation each day.

Stars look small.
They are far away.
The Sun is the closest star to Earth.

Part of Earth faces the Sun.

Then it is day.

Part of Earth faces away from the Sun.

Then it is night.

Rotation makes day and night.

Most planets are hard to see.

You can use a telescope.

A **telescope** makes things that are far away look closer.

What is in the night sky?

Stars are in the sky.

A **star** is a big ball of hot gas.

Stars give off light.

Stars seem to move across the sky.

Earth is a **planet.**

Nine planets move around the Sun.

Planets do not give off light.

Science

Science in Our World

by Zachary Cohn

Genre	Comprehension Skill	Text Features	Science Content
Nonfiction	Put Things in Order	• Captions • Glossary	Technology

Scott Foresman Science 1.12

PEARSON

Scott Foresman

scottforesman.com

111

What did you learn?

1. Where does food come from?

2. What are simple machines? Name some simple machines and describe what they do.

3. **Writing** in Science Tools make doing jobs faster and easier. Write to describe some of the tools used to make and serve dinner. Use words from the book as you write.

4. **Put Things in Order** What happens to a tree before it is cut in a mill?

Photographs: Every effort has been made to secure permission and provide appropriate credit for photographic material. The publisher deeply regrets any omission and pledges to correct errors called to its attention in subsequent editions. Unless otherwise acknowledged, all photographs are the property of Scott Foresman, a division of Pearson Education. Photo locators denoted as follows: Top (T), Center (C), Bottom (B), Left (L), Right (R) Background (Bkgd)
Opener: ©Peter Beck/Corbis; 2 ©M. H. Black/Robert Harding Picture Library Ltd., ©Randy Wells/Corbis; 3 ©DK Images; 4 ©Sylvain Saustier/Corbis; 5 ©Ken Wagner/Visuals Unlimited, (TR) ©Eric and David Hosking/Corbis; 6 ©Byron Jorjorian/Bruce Coleman Inc.; 7 ©Stone/Getty Images; 10 ©Grant Heilman Photography; 12 ©Royalty-Free/Corbis; 14 (BC, CR) ©Royalty-Free/Corbis

ISBN: 0-328-13766-9

Glossary

inclined plane   a simple machine that is high at one end and low at the other end

lever   a simple machine that is used to lift something

pulley   a simple machine that uses a wheel and rope to move things up and down

screw   a simple machine that is used to hold things together

simple machine   a tool with few or no moving parts that makes work easier

technology   the use of scientific knowledge to solve problems

wedge   a simple machine that is used to push things apart

wheel and axle   a simple machine that is used to move things

Science in Our World

by Zachary Cohn

How do farmers use technology to grow food?

Food comes from many places.

Food comes from lakes.

Food comes from animals.

Food comes from farms.

What can you use to communicate?

Computers are technology.

Technology is used to communicate.

The ways we communicate have changed.

Using Simple Machines

A **screw** holds things together.

A **lever** lifts things.

A **pulley** moves things up
and down.

An **inclined plane** has one high
end and one low end.

Machines help farmers.

Machines are technology.

Technology is using science to
solve problems.

Technology changes with time.

Planting and Growing Corn

The farmer plows the soil.

The plow makes the job easier.

The plow is technology.

The soil is ready to plant.

A **wedge** is a simple machine.

It pushes things apart.

A **wheel and axle** is a simple machine.

It moves things.

This wheelbarrow has a wheel and axle.

This shovel is a wedge.

What are simple machines?

People use simple machines.

A **simple machine** is a tool.

It has few or no moving parts.

Simple machines help do jobs.

The farmer plants seeds.

The farmer uses a seed drill.

A seed drill is technology.

It makes the work go faster.

How does food get from the farm to the store?

The corn plants grow.

The farmer picks the corn.

This is called a harvest.

Machines help the farmer.

Moving Logs to the Sawmill

This machine picks up the logs.

It places them on the truck.

The truck goes to the mill.

The logs are cut in the mill.

How do builders get wood
for a house?

Workers used axes long ago.

Now they use machines.

One machine cuts the trees.

One moves the heavy logs.

The corn is ready to sell.

It is put on a truck.

The truck takes the corn to the store.

What tools can you use to make dinner?

People use tools.

Tools make work easier.

Each tool is used for a different job.

Serving Dinner

We need tools to make dinner.

What will you use?

A spoon can lift the meat.

Tongs can pick up lettuce.